Remembering Seattle

Walt Crowley

TURNER
PUBLISHING COMPANY

Men and women on West Seattle shoreline.

Remembering
Seattle

Turner Publishing Company
www.turnerpublishing.com

Remembering Seattle

Copyright © 2010 Turner Publishing Company

Library of Congress Control Number: 2010902290

ISBN: 978-1-59652-616-7

Printed in the United States of America

ISBN: 978-1-68336-883-0 (pbk.)

CONTENTS

Hotel at Woodland Park in 1891.

Acknowledgments

This volume, *Remembering Seattle,* is the result of the cooperation and efforts of many individuals and organizations. It is with great thanks that we acknowledge the valuable contribution of the following for their generous support:

Seattle Municipal Archives

University of Washington Libraries Digital Collections

The Edgewater Hotel

The Roosevelt Hotel

We would also like to thank Walt Crowley, author and editor, for his valuable contributions and assistance in making this work possible.

PREFACE

Seattle has thousands of historic photographs that reside in archives, both locally and nationally. This book began with the observation that, while those photographs are of great interest to many, some are not easily accessible. During a time when Seattle is looking ahead and evaluating its future course, many people are asking, How do we treat the past? These decisions affect every aspect of the city—architecture, public spaces, commerce, infrastructure—and these, in turn, affect the way that people live their lives. This book seeks to provide easy access to a valuable, objective look into the history of Seattle.

The power of photographs is that they are less subjective than words in their treatment of history. Although the photographer can make subjective decisions regarding subject matter and how to capture and present it, photographs seldom interpret the past to the extent textual histories can. For this reason, photography is uniquely positioned to offer an original, untainted look at the past, allowing the viewer to learn for himself what the world was like a century or more ago.

This project represents countless hours of review and research. The researchers and writer have reviewed thousands of photographs in numerous archives. We greatly appreciate the generous assistance of the archives listed in the acknowledgments of this work, without whom this project could not have been completed.

The goal in publishing this work is to provide broader access to this set of extraordinary photographs that seek to inspire, provide perspective, and evoke insight that might assist people who are responsible for determining Seattle's future. In addition, the book seeks to preserve the past with adequate respect and reverence.

With the exception of touching up imperfections that have accrued with the passage of time and cropping where necessary, no changes have been made. The focus and clarity of many images are limited to the technology and the ability of the photographer at the time they were recorded.

The work is divided into eras. Beginning with some of the earliest known photographs of Seattle, the first section records photographs from the late nineteenth century. The second section spans the beginning of the twentieth century through World War I. Section Three moves into the era between the world wars, and Section Four takes a look at the World War II and postwar eras.

In each of these sections we have made an effort to capture various aspects of life through our selection of photographs. People, commerce, transportation, infrastructure, religious institutions, and educational institutions have been included to provide a broad perspective.

We encourage readers to reflect as they go walking in Seattle, strolling through the city, its parks, and its neighborhoods. It is the publisher's hope that in utilizing this work, longtime residents will learn something new and that new residents will gain a perspective on where Seattle has been, so that each can contribute to its future.

—Todd Bottorff, Publisher

Pioneer Square, from waterfront looking up Yesler. The Seattle Hotel is in the center.

Planting the Seeds

(1880s–1899)

This trolley traveled around the east side of Green Lake. (1897)

Leschi Park. (1895)

Cedar River Pipeline No. 1 being laid up Bagley Hill near Renton. (1899)

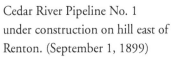
Cedar River Pipeline No. 1 under construction on hill east of Renton. (September 1, 1899)

This photo was taken the day after the Seattle fire of June 6, 1889. The *Seattle Daily Press* newspaper staff and equipment are housed in a temporary tent.

The big fire of June 6, 1889, looking south on First Avenue from Spring Street. This is about half an hour after the fire started. In the background the Frye's Opera House is starting to burn.

Lodge at left entrance (Fremont Avenue) of Woodland Park.

Fremont Avenue entrance, Woodland Park. Owner, Guy Carlton Phinney. (1891)

Sullivan Building at right with the Starr-Boyd Building. The cable car turning onto First Avenue is one from the Front Street Cable Runway.

Woodland Park looking south toward Fremont Avenue entrance from hotel. (1891)

Guy Phinney's private streetcar connected his Woodland Park resort to Fremont.

Native American camp at the foot of Washington Street on Ballast Island. (1891)

Digging a trench in the bottom of Black River to construct Cedar River Pipeline No. 1. (1899)

Lincoln Park Reservoir under construction. (1899)

A Tlingit totem pole was erected at Pioneer Place, First Avenue and Yesler Way, in 1899. (shown here in 1904; since replaced).

GOLDEN DECADES

(1900–1919)

Construction of the Great Northern Railroad tunnel beneath downtown Seattle. (1903)

Lake Washington, Madison Park. (May 1903)

Leschi Park. (1906)

Cedar River Watershed.

Engine House No. 25 at E. Union Street. (1910)

Waterfront Fire Station on Madison Street. (1910)

Woodland Park. (1910)

Pike Place Market looking west down Pike Street. (1910)

Fire Department Headquarters at Columbia Street between 6th and 7th avenues. (1910)

Broadway Playfield.

Engine House No. 8 and stand pipe on Queen Anne Hill.

Waterfront Fire Station with fireboats *Snoqualmie* and *Duwamish*. (1910)

Schmitz Park. (1910)

Pike Place, Corner of Pike Street, Pike Place, and First Avenue in 1910, before erection of Corner Market Building.

New-style drinking fountain, 7th and Jackson.
(1911)

Playground units in the First Golden Potlatch Parade. (1911)

The First Golden Potlatch Parade marches on Second Avenue.

Bathing at Alki Beach. (1911)

Bathhouse and pavilion, Alki Beach.

Alki Beach.

Interlaken Boulevard, just south of Seattle Preparatory. The University of Washington campus and buildings are just across the bay. (1911)

Northern view of 2nd Avenue from Madison Street showing the regrade work. (1914)

Meter Testing Room, Seattle Lighting Company. (1913)

Three men on a small engine on a track at Masonry Dam. The sign reads "The Municipal Light and Power Plant of Seattle America's Best Lighted City 40 miles."

Lander Street Terminal. East Waterway Just North of Lander Street. (1914)

Repaving Second Avenue at the intersection of Columbia.

Southeast corner of Maynard Avenue and Main Street. (1915)

East Waterway Terminal, Hanford Street Terminal.

Checking scales at the main arcade interior stalls.

Workers paving the Fremont Avenue Bridge. (1917)

Pike Place Market looking south on Pike Place toward Pike Street. (1919)

Between the Wars

(1920–1939)

Lincoln Hotel between Third and Fourth on the north side of Madison.

Produce and meat vendors.

Women working in Crescent Manufacturing Company. (1920)

Harbormaster's dock at foot of Washington Street. (ca. 1930)

A view down Western Avenue showing construction of the addition to Main Market and bridges.

Seattle Public Safety Building (center) on Yesler Way circa 1920. Tower on left is old King County Courthouse.

Removing snow from streets of Seattle following the storm of February 14, 1923.

Heavy snowfall required heavy lifting.

Meat market interior.

Ben Evans ("Old Woody") and gang at Rogers playfield. (1924)

Onlookers of auto accident at Railroad Avenue on the Port of Seattle. (1925)

Special newsstand at southwest corner of 4th Avenue and Pike Street.

Placing Amiesite at 7th Avenue South and Dearborn Street.

New Richelieu Hotel and Shorey's Bookstore on Third Avenue. (1929)

Seattle waterfront and boats near Schwabacher's Wharf at Pier 7.

Second Avenue at Jackson.

Highway Fruit Company with billboard featuring the Coca-Cola trademark. (1930)

Denny Regrade Fourth Avenue and Blanchard. (1930)

Third Avenue North from Marion showing Oxford Tailoring Company, Raymer's Books, Hotel Albany, and the Pacific Coast China Company. (1930)

Meat market.

Youngstown Place streetcar viaduct, West Seattle. (1930)

Railroad Avenue (now Alaskan Way) on central waterfront. (1930)

Youngstown Place. (1930)

Youngstown Place venues. (1930)

Mayor Frank Edwards at Diablo Dam dedication, City Light Skagit River Project. (1930)

Diablo Dam incline railway, Seattle City Light Skagit River Project. (1930)

West Garfield Street Bridge.

Street department equipment display.

Pike Place Market, meat stall.

West Seattle Reservoir under construction.

Three Girls Bakery was in the corner of the Corner Market building from 1912 to 1933.

Streetcars at Second and Pike.

Pike Place Market, Main Arcade. (1936)

Port of Seattle's Fishermen's Terminal, Salmon Bay.

Salmon Bay Terminal, Port of Seattle. (1936)

Alki Beach. (1936)

Lincoln Park, West Seattle.

Lincoln Park on the waterfront, West Seattle.

Constructing Devil's Elbow Bridge, Seattle City Light Skagit River Project. (1936)

Men at work on snow slide above Devil's Elbow Bridge. (1936)

Traffic Control Board at the City-County Building. (1936)

Fourth of July parade, City Hall Park. The Frye Hotel stands in the background.

James Wehn's sculpture of Chief Seattle at Tilikum Place, Fifth Avenue and Denny Way.

Shrine Parade on Second Avenue.

Byron Hotel. (1937)

Triangle Building with McDonald's Grocery and Bakery and Market Apartments. (1937)

Fourth Avenue trackless trolley wires between Columbia and Marion streets.

Second and Pike streets. (1938)

Ross Dam Construction, Seattle
City Light Skagit River Project.

Looking north on Fourth Avenue from Pike Street. (1939)

Ben Paris Kitchen.

Homeless shantytown known as Hooverville. (1937)

Seattle Carefree Cooks Club.

DOOM AND BOOM

(1940–1970s)

Seattle Model Yacht Club at Golden Gardens.

Camp Long dedication. (November 8, 1941)

West Seattle branch war bonds promotion. "Buy War Bonds– Back the Attack."

Bob Hope at Victory Square.

West Seattle Golf Course.

Newsstand, Third and Pike. (1946)

Alki Beach "duck," operated by J. F. Boles of Puget Sound Log Patrol.

West Myrtle Street Reservoir under construction.

Garland Florist between Tenth and Twelfth on Jackson Street.

Mount Baker Bathing Beach.

Engine no. 6, Seattle City Light Skagit River Project.

View of Seattle skyline from Belvedere Place, West Seattle, featuring Bella Coola totem pole.

Vann Brothers Restaurant.

Skagit River no. 6 steam engine.

The Northern Lights Dining Room,
1125 3rd Avenue.

The Northern Lights Dining Room, 1125 3rd Avenue.

Alaskan Way Viaduct, South End.

Chuck and Terry's Fish and Chips.

Volunteer Park, Seattle Art Museum.

Trackless trolley stop on Pike Street at Fourth Avenue. (ca. 1954)

Trackless trolleys on Pike Street at Fourth Avenue. (ca. 1954)

Roll-out of Dash-80 prototype of the Boeing 707 jetliner, Boeing Field. (1954)

Jackson Park Golf Course.

One of the several Skagit River hydroelectric projects, the Ross Dam created the waters of Ross Lake.

Belvedere Place viewpoint. (1965)

Corner of Pike Street and First Avenue.

Looking west over downtown Seattle and the Century 21 Exhibition site.

NOTES ON THE PHOTOGRAPHS

These notes, listed by page number, attempt to include all aspects known of the photographs. Each of the photographs is identified by the page number, a title or description, photographer and collection, archive, and call or box number when applicable. Although every attempt was made to collect all data, in some cases complete data may have been unavailable due to the age and condition of some of the photographs and records.